DEATH
AND
BEREAVEMENT

Death and Bereavement

Four talks given at the Russian Orthodox Cathedral of the Dormition and All Saints, Ennismore Gardens, London, in April and May 1984

by

Metropolitan Anthony of Sourozh

****

St Stephen's Press

Published by
St Stephen's Press
PO Box 47 Oxford OX2 6LW
ssp@sourozh.org

© 2002 Metropolitan Anthony of Sourozh

ISBN 0 951 9037 9 9

Cover photograph by Nick Hale

Printed by Will Print, Oxford

DEATH AND BEREAVEMENT

CONTENTS

Remembrance of Death 1

Personal Reminiscences 13

Bereavement 25

Death 37

REMEMBRANCE OF DEATH

To begin with, I would like to dispel, if I can, the habitual attitude which modern man has developed concerning death – a feeling of fear, of rejection, the feeling that death is the worst that can occur to a person and that at all costs survival must be achieved, even if survival has little to do with real living.

In earlier times when Christians were nearer to both their pagan roots and the tremendous, overwhelming experience of conversion, of the discovery of the Living God in and through Christ, death was spoken of in terms of a birth into eternal life. It was perceived not as an end, not as the ultimate defeat, but as a beginning. Life was thought of as an ascent towards eternity, and death was felt to be that door which opens and allows us to enter it. This explains why so often the early Christians used to remind one another of death with words like 'Remember death', while in the prayers which St John Chrysostom has left us as a precious inheritance there is a petition in which we ask God to give us ' remembrance of death'. When such words are spoken to modern man, the reaction is usually one of rejection, of revulsion. Do we mean by such words that we must remember that death is there like the sword of Damocles over our heads, hanging over us on a hair, that at any moment the banquet of life may end horribly, tragically? Does it mean that whenever joy comes our way we must be aware that it will have an end? Is it that we wish to darken the light of every day by fear of an impending death?

This is not what the early Christian felt. What he felt was that death is a decisive moment at which all that we can do on earth will have come to an end and that we must hurry; we must hurry to achieve on earth all that can be achieved. All this was, paradoxically, an aim to achieve in life – particularly in the minds of spiritual guides: to become the true person whom we were called by God to be, to reach as near as we can to what St Paul calls the full stature of Christ, to become as perfectly as possible an undistorted image of God.

St Paul says that we must make haste to live because time is deceptive. And indeed is time not deceptive? Do we not we live all the days of our life as though we were writing hastily, carelessly, a draft of the life which one day we would copy out in a fair hand, as though we were just preparing to build, collecting all that would later be organised into beauty, into harmony, into meaning? We live this way year after year, not doing completely, fully, perfectly, what we could do, because there is time ahead of us; later we will achieve something; later it can be done; one day a fair copy will be written. Years pass and we never do it. We never do it, not only because death comes and harvests us, but because at every period of life we become unable to do what the previous period would have allowed us to do. It is not in our mature years that we can achieve a beautiful and meaningful youth, as it is not in old age that we can reveal to God and to the world what we might have been in years of our maturity. There is a time for all things, but once the time has gone, these things can no longer be done.

I have quoted, on more than one occasion, words of Victor Hugo, who said that there is fire in the eyes of the young; but there should be light in the eyes of the old. The time of glowing fire passes, the time of light reaches us, but when the time of being a light has come, we no longer can do those things which can be done only in the days of our flaming. The days that pass are deceptive. Time is deceptive. And when we are told that we must remember death, it is not in order to give us a fear of life; it is in order to make us live with all the intensity we would have if we were aware that every moment is the only moment which we possess and that each moment, every single moment of our life, must be not a trough, but the crest of a wave, not a defeat but a triumph. When I speak of defeat and triumph I do not mean outward success or lack of it. I mean an inner achievement, growth, an ability to be perfectly and fully what we are at a given moment.

Think what every moment of our life would be like if we were aware that it may be the last one, that this moment is given us to reach some kind of perfection, that the words which we speak will be our last, so they must express all the beauty, all the wisdom, all the knowledge, and indeed most of all, all the love which we have learnt in the course of our lives, whether they be short or long. How would we act with regard to each other if the present moment were the only moment at our disposal and if this moment had to express, to embody all that there is in us of love, of concern? We would live with an intensity and a depth which otherwise we would never achieve. And yet we are hardly aware of what this present moment is. We move from the past into the future without ever really living intensely at the present moment.

In his diary, Dostoevsky speaks to us of what happened to him when, being condemned to death, he stood, about to be shot, and how he looked around himself. How glorious the light was and how wonderful the air he was breathing and how beautiful was the world around him, how precious was every moment during which he was still alive while he was on the brink of death. 'Oh', he says at that moment, 'if life were given me, not one moment of it would be wasted.' Life was given, and so much of it was wasted!

If we were aware of this, how would we treat one another, and indeed ourselves? If I was aware, if you were aware, that the person to whom you speak may die within moments and that the sound of your voice, the content of your words, your gestures, your intentions, the way you relate to that person, will be the last things to be perceived and taken into eternity – how thoughtful, how careful, indeed how loving we would be. Experience shows that in the face of death so many resentments, so much bitterness, so much mutual rejection dies out. Death is too great for things which should be too small even for temporary life.

And so death, the thought of it, the remembrance of it, seems to be the only power that makes life ultimately intense: to live up to death, to live in such a way that death may come at any moment and meet us on the crest of the wave, not in the trough, that our last words should not have been a jarring cry or our last gesture a careless movement. Those of us who have had occasion to live for a certain time with a dying person, with a person aware of the coming of death, a death of which we too were aware, have understood what the presence of death can mean in a relationship. It means that every word must contain all the reverence, all the beauty, all the harmony and love which was perhaps dormant within the relationship. It means that there is nothing which is small, because everything, however small, can be an expression of love, or a denial of it.

This is very important, because it colours the whole of our attitude to death. It may make it a great challenge, something that allows us to grow to our full stature and continuously to try to be all that we can be, without any hope of doing better later if we do not care to do the right thing today. Dostoevsky again, in *The Brothers Karamazov*, speaks of hell, which he says can be summed up in two words: too late! Only remembrance of death can allow us so to live that we should never be confronted with this terrifying phrase and the frightful awareness: that it is too late. Words that could be spoken, gestures that could fulfil a relationship can no longer be spoken, can no longer be made. This does not mean that ultimately this cannot be achieved, but in another way, at the cost of much pain, of much agony of mind.

I would like to illustrate this point and make it clearer. Some years ago, an old man in his mid-eighties came to see me. He wanted advice because he could not continue to live in the agony that had been his for some sixty years. In the course of the Civil War in Russia he had killed the girl whom he loved and who loved him dearly. They intended to marry, but in the course of the shooting she had suddenly run across his line of fire and it was too late to deflect his shot. For sixty years he could not find peace. Not only had he cut short a life that was infinitely precious to him, but one that was blossoming and that was infinitely precious to the girl he loved.

He told me that he had prayed, begged forgiveness of the Lord, had gone to confession, made penance, received absolution and Communion – done everything which his imagination and the imagination of those to whom he turned suggested – but he could never find peace. In the inspiration of an intense, searing sympathy and compassion I said to him, 'You can turn to Christ whom you have not murdered, to priests whom you have not harmed. Why haven't you ever thought of turning to the girl that you killed?' He was surprised. Cannot God forgive? Is He not the only one who can forgive the sins of men on earth? And indeed, of course, it is so. But I suggested to him that if the girl whom he had shot could forgive, could intercede for him, even God could not pass her by.

There is a passage in the Book of Daniel in which we are told that Daniel prayed, and God said to him that his prayer was in vain because an old woman who had a grudge against him was praying against his prayer and that her prayer was like a strong wind that dispersed like smoke the prayer which he hoped would ascend to heaven. Perhaps this was the image, that came to me subconsciously.

I suggested to him that he should sit down after evening prayers and tell this girl about these sixty years of mental agony, of a heart laid to waste, of the pain he had endured, ask her forgiveness and then ask her also to intercede for him and to ask the Lord to send peace into his heart if she had forgiven. And he did it, and peace came. So what is left undone on earth can be fulfilled. What has been a failure on earth can later be healed, but years of pain and remorse, of tears and loneliness, may be the price.

When we think of death, we should not think of it as either a glorious or a miserable event. The vision which God gives of it in the Bible and in the Gospels is more complex than that. To put it briefly: God did not create us for death, for destruction. He created us for eternal life. He called us to immortality – not only to the immortality of the resurrection, but to an immortality that knew no death. Death came as the result of sin. It came because man lost God, turned away from Him, looked for ways in which he could achieve all things without God. The knowledge which could have been acquired by communion with the knowledge and wisdom of God man tried to acquire himself. Instead of living in the familiarity of God, he chose his own independence. The French pastor, Roland de Curie, suggests what is perhaps a good image: that the moment man turned his back on God and looked into the infinite in front of him, there was no God for him; and as God is the only source of life, he could do nothing but die.

If we look in the Bible, we will find something striking in the destiny of mankind. Death came, but it did not conquer mankind suddenly in the same way in which it conquered him later. Whatever the objective figures that indicate the length of days in the life of the first ten great generations in the Bible, we can see that the length of days diminishes gradually. There are passages in the Bible that make it clear that death conquered mankind step by step. Death had come, but the power of life was still there; but gradually, from one generation to another of mortal and sinful men, death increasingly reduced the lifespan of mankind. So there is tragedy in death. On the one hand, death is monstrous; death should not be there at all. Death is the result of our loss of God. On the other hand, there is another aspect of death. An endless duration of separateness from God, thousands and thousands of years of life without any hope that there will be an end to this separation from God would be more horrible than the dissolution of our bodily frame and an end to this vicious circle.

And then there is another aspect of death: narrow as the gate is, it is the only gate that allows us to escape from the vicious circle of endlessness apart from God, apart from fulfilment, a creaturely endlessness in which there is no space for our becoming again partakers in the life of God and ultimately partakers of the divine nature. This is why St Paul could say: 'For me to live is Christ. Death will be a gain, because as long as I live in this body I am separated from Christ.' This is why he said in another passage that for him to die is not to divest himself of this temporary life: for him, to die means to be clothed in eternity. It is not an end; it is a beginning. It is a door that opens and allows us into the vastness of eternity which would be closed for us for ever if death did not free us from our integration into earthly things.

In our attitude to death these two aspects must each play a role. When a person dies we can legitimately be heartbroken. We can look with horror at the fact that sin has murdered a person whom we love. We can deny the fact that we accept death as the last word, the last event in life. We are right when we weep over the departed, because this should not be. He or she was killed by evil. On the other hand we can rejoice for the person who has died because new life, unbounded, free, has begun for him or her. And again, we can weep for ourselves, our bereavement, our loneliness, but at the same time we must learn what the

Old Testament had already foreseen: 'Love is as strong as death' (Song of Solomon, 8:6), the love that does not allow the memory of the beloved to fade, the love that makes us speak of our relationship with the beloved one not in the past tense: 'I loved him, we were so close,' but makes us think in the present tense: 'I love her; we are so close.'

In the New Testament we find something even greater than this, because with the resurrection of Christ, death is virtually overcome. It is overcome because we know through the resurrection of Christ, that death is not the last word and that we are called to rise again and to live. Death is also defeated in the victory of Christ over sin and over death itself in the harrowing of hell, because the most horrible aspect of death, as it was conceived in the Old Testament by the people of Israel, was that the state of separation from God that had brought about death was made definitive, unconquerable, by death itself.

Those who had died – and this applied to everyone – those who had died of the loss of God in death lost him for ever. The Old Testament *Sheol* was the place where God is not, the place of definitive, irrevocable absence and separation. In the resurrection of Christ, in His descent into hell and the harrowing of hell, this has come to an end. There is separation on earth and the pain of separation, but there is no separation in death from God. On the contrary, death is the moment and the way in which, however separate, however incompletely united or in harmony with God we may have been, we present ourselves before His face. God is the Saviour of the world. Did He not say more than once: 'I have come not to judge the world but to save the world'? We stand before Him who is salvation.

So there is complexity in death – one might even say an ambiguity – but we have no right, if we are Christ's own people, to allow ourselves to overlook the birth into eternity of the departing one because we ourselves are so deeply wounded by our bereavement and overcome by our earthly loneliness. There is in death a power of life that reaches out to us. If our love is faithful, if we are capable of remembering, not only with our mind but with our heart, those whom we have loved on earth, then, as Christ puts it, 'Where your treasure is, there will your heart be also', and through the death of loved ones we are, as it were, already to a certain extent in that eternity which they inhabit. If our hearts are faithful, we are already together with them but, at the same time, if their lives have meant something to us, if their lives have been an example or a warning, we can continue to live, not in separation, but in continuity with them.

We can live to their redemption and their glory. We can live embodying in all our life all that was meaningful, noble and true in them, so that one day, when the time comes for us also to stand before God, together with the whole of mankind, we can offer to the Lord all the fruits, all the harvest of the seeds which were sown by their example, by their lives, and which grew and fructified thanks to the undying love which we possess. We can say to the Lord: 'Take all this from me; it belongs to him, to her. I am only a field; he was the sower! Her example, her words, her person were like seed spread on this earth, and now the harvest which has come belongs to her.'

****

PERSONAL REMINSCENCES

It is difficult, if not impossible, to speak of questions of life and death without being personal, perhaps more than some would wish. We meet death in our lives, first of all, not as a subject on which we reflect – although this does happen - but mainly as a result of bereavement, either our own or someone else's. It is this vicarious experience of death that serves as a background for us to reflect afterwards on the certainty of our own death, and on the way in which we relate to it. I will begin with a few examples of the way in which I personally have met other people's deaths, and that will perhaps explain to you my own attitude to it.

My first reminiscence of death goes very far back, to a moment when I was still a child in Persia. One evening, as was the custom at that time, my parents took me to visit the rose garden of a man who was renowned for the beauty of his flowers. We arrived and were received by the master of the house and his household. We were taken around his most beautiful gardens, invited to share refreshments, and sent home with a sense of having enjoyed the warmest, the most open-hearted and the least constrained hospitality one could imagine. It was only on the next day that we discovered that while we were going around with the master of the house, admiring his flowers, being treated to refreshments, entertained with all the courtesy of the Orient, his son, who had been murdered a few hours before, was lying in one of the rooms of the house. And this, small though I was, gave me a very strong sense of what life and death are, and what is the duty of those who are alive to other people who are alive, whatever the circumstances.

My second memory is that of a conversation, during the Civil War, or towards the end of the First World War, between two young women; the brother of the one, who was the bridegroom of the other, had been killed. The news reached the bride. She came to her friend, the sister and said to her, 'Rejoice, your brother has died heroically, fighting for his country.' This again gave me a measure of the greatness of the human soul, of the vastness which human courage could possess, the ability to stand up not only to danger, to suffering and to life in all its manifold aspects, all its complexity, but to the simplicity and sharpness of death.

A few more memories. When I was a teenager I came back from summer camp. My father met me and expressed his worry about the way in which the camp had been run. 'I thought,' he said, 'something had happened to you.' Flippantly, I said, 'Did you expect me to have broken a leg or my neck?', and very earnestly he said, with the sober love that was so characteristic of him, 'No, this would have mattered little. I was afraid you had lost your integrity.' And then he went on to say, 'Remember that whether you live or die is of little importance. What really matters, and should matter both to you and to others, is what you live for, and what you are prepared to die for.'

This again gave me a measure of life, and a vision of what life should be in relation to death, the ultimate challenge to learn to live in such a way, as he said to me at another moment, that you should wait for your own death as a young man awaits his bride, to wait for death to come as the beloved one, to wait for a door to open.

I come now to a thought that requires a great deal more reflection than I have done, but something which I experienced almost violently in my heart in the course of this Holy Week – if Christ is the Door which opens on to eternity, He is our death. This could be substantiated formally by the passage from the Epistle to the Romans which we read at Baptism (Romans 6: 3-11), where it is said that we are merged in the death of Christ in order to rise with Him. And also by another passage which says that we carry in our bodies the deadness of Christ. He is death and He is life itself and the resurrection.

And then a last image: the death of my father. He was a shy man. He spoke little, and we spoke little to one another. On Easter Day he felt unwell for a short moment, so he lay down. I sat next to him and for the first time in our lives we spoke with total openness. It was not our words that were so significant. There was an openness of mind and heart. The doors had opened. Silence was as open and as deep as the words. And then I had to go. I said goodbye to everyone who was in the room, but not to him, because I felt that, having met as we had met, we could not ever part from one another. There was no goodbye. There was not even an '*au revoir*', a 'See you again'; we had met, and that was for ever. He died the same night. I remember coming back from the hospital where I worked, being told that he had died, walking to his room and shutting the door behind me. What I experienced was a quality and depth of silence that was not to any degree an absence of noise, an absence of sound. It was a silence that was substantial, 'a silence', as the French writer Georges Bernanos said in one of his novels, 'that was a presence'. And I heard myself say, 'And people dare to say that death exists. What a lie.'

I bring to you these examples for you to understand why my attitude to death is perhaps so one-sided, why I see the glory of it, and not only the pain and the bereavement. I do see the pain and the bereavement. These examples which I have given you refer to sudden death, to unexpected death, the death that comes like the 'thief in the night'. This is not what usually happens. But if such experiences as I have given you come your way, you will probably understand how even while one's heart is in searing pain and agony, one can still rejoice, and how – to this we will come later – how in our funeral service we can exclaim: 'Blessed is the road which thou treadest today, O human soul, because a place of refreshment is prepared for thee', and why we use the words of a psalm in the same service earlier, as though the departed were speaking to us saying, 'My soul lives and I give glory unto the Lord.'

But more often than with sudden death we are confronted with long or short terminal illnesses and with old age that brings us gradually either to our grave – seen from one viewpoint – or to our freedom: the supreme encounter which each of us, knowingly or unknowingly, longs and strives for throughout our earthly life, our meeting face to face with the Living God, our encounter with Life eternal, our communion with Him. So this period of illness or of increasing old age must be faced and must be understood creatively, usefully.

One of the great tragedies of life which brings great agony of mind and torment to people is when they see a beloved person grow older and older, lose his or her physical and mental faculties, seeming to lose what was most precious: a clear mind, a witty, ever ready response to life. So often this process is ignored, overlooked. We close our eyes so as not to see, because we are afraid of seeing – and foreseeing – and the result is that when death comes, it is a sudden death which not only has all the horror of an unexpected death, but has the additional horror of hitting us in our most vulnerable state, because the pain, the fear, the anguish have been growing in intensity within us while we were refusing to give them freedom of expression and any possibility of maturity. The blow is even more painful, more destructive than that of sudden death because then, together with the horror, the pain of bereavement, comes all the self-reproach and self-condemnation for not having done all that could have been done because to do it would have forced us to confront the truth, would have forced us into honesty and into an unveiling for ourselves and for the aged or dying person of the fact that death was gradually opening a door, and that this door would one day open wide and the beloved one would have to enter into it without even looking back.

It is important for all of us, whenever we are confronted with this gradually approaching bereavement, to face it from the beginning and to face it in the wonderfully balanced way in which we can do it while the person is still alive and in our midst. For over against the thought of the coming death there is the reality of a living presence. We can constantly lean on the security of this presence while we become more and more aware of the complexity of the coming bereavement. It is this balance between the power of reality and the frailty of thought that makes it possible for us to prepare ourselves for the death of people who are precious to us.

This preparation, of course, also entails an attitude to death which recognises on the one hand the horror and the pain of bereavement, but at the same time the fact that it is a door opening into life eternal. 'To me to die is not to divest myself of temporal life, but to clothe myself in eternity,' said St Paul. This period of preparation I will also illustrate with a couple of examples. The first reflects the importance of breaking down barriers, of not allowing fear to build a wall of partition between the dying person and ourselves, so that the person who is dying is condemned to loneliness, is condemned to be abandoned, to struggle against all that death may mean to him or to her without any support or understanding. This fear can also create a barrier that prevents us from doing all we could so that no rancour, no self-reproach or despair is left behind.

We cannot lightly say to a person, 'Beware, you will soon die.' In order to be able to face death one must be anchored in the certainty, an experiential and not only theoretical certainty, of eternal life. And so when we see the first signs of the coming of death we must work intelligently, systematically, to make the person who will enter into its mystery discover what life eternal is, to help them see to what extent this eternal life is something they already possess, the fact that there is in this possession of eternal life a certainty that reduces to nought the fear of death – not the pain of separation, not the regret that death exists, but the fear. There are people to whom one can say, 'Death is here: let us go hand in hand into the experience of dying. And let us go together into the degree of communion in eternity which will be accessible to each of us.'

My mother died of cancer over a period of three years. She was operated on unsuccessfully. The doctor told me about this and then added, 'But of course you will not say anything to your mother.' I said, 'I will.' And I did. I remember how I came to her and said to her that her doctor had rung and that the operation was not successful. We kept silence for a moment, and then my mother said, 'And so I shall die.' And I said, 'Yes.' And then we stayed together in complete silence, communing without any words. I do not think that we thought any thoughts. We faced something that had entered our lives and made all the difference to them. It was not a shadow. It was not an evil. It was not a terror. It was the ultimate, and we had to face this ultimate without yet knowing what this ultimate would unfold into. We stayed as long as we felt we had to stay. And then life continued.

But two things happened as a result. One was that at no moment was either my mother or I walled up within a lie, forced into a comedy, deprived of help. At no moment did I have to come into my mother's room with a smile that was untrue, or say words that were untrue. At no moment did we have to play a comedy of life conquering death, of illness waning, of things being better than they were, when we both knew they were not. At no moment were we deprived of one another's help. She would ring the bell and I would come and we would speak of her dying, of my bereavement. She loved life and loved it deeply. A few days before she died she said that she would be prepared to live a hundred and fifty years in suffering, but to live. She loved the beauty of spring, which was coming. She loved us. She grieved over separation: 'O, for the touch of a vanished hand and the sound of a voice that is still.' And then there were other moments when I felt the pain of it, and I would come and speak of it to my mother. And she would give me her support and help me face her death. This was a deep and true relationship. There was nothing of a lie in it. And, therefore, all that was true could find a place in it.

Because death was there, because at any moment death could come and it would be too late to put right anything that had gone wrong, at every moment all of life had to be an expression, as perfect and complete as possible, of a relationship that was a relationship of reverence and love. Only death can make things that seem to be so small, so insignificant, into signs that are great and significant: the way a cup of tea is prepared on a tray, the way one puts cushions behind the back of a sick person, the way your voice sounds, the way you move – all that can be an expression of all the fullness of a relationship. If there is a false note, if there is a crack, if something has gone wrong, it must be repaired immediately, because there is the inevitable certainty that it may soon be too late. Again this confronts us with the truth of life, with a sharpness, with a clarity, that nothing else can.

It is very important, as I said earlier, whether we face our own death or the death of another person, for us to become aware of eternity. Some thirty years ago, a man was taken to hospital with, as it seemed, a common illness. On examination it was discovered that he was suffering from an inoperable and incurable cancer. His sister was told, and so was I, but he was not. He was in bed, vigorous, strong, intensely alive. He said to me: 'I have so much to do, and here I am, bedridden, and for how long?' I said to him, 'How often have you told me that you dream of being able to stop time so that you can *be* instead of doing. You have never done it. God has done it for you. Now is your time to *be*.' And confronted with the necessity of being, in what one might call a totally contemplative situation, he was puzzled and said, 'What shall I do?'

I said to him that illness and death are conditioned not only by physiological changes, by germs, by pathology, but also by all those things which destroy our inner energies, by what one may call our negative feelings and negative thoughts, everything that saps the power of life within us, prevents life from gushing like a torrent clear and free. And so I suggested that he should put right – not only outwardly but within himself – all that was wrong in his relationships with people, with himself, with what had gone wrong in the circumstances of his life. He should begin with the present moment; and when he had done it in the present, he should go back and back into the past, clearing all his past, making his peace with everyone and everything, undoing every knot, facing every evil, coming to terms in repentance, in acceptance, in gratitude, with all his life; and his life had been hard.

So month after month, day after day, we went through this process. He made his peace with the totality of life. And I can remember him at the end of it, lying in his bed too weak to use a spoon, and saying to me with shining eyes, 'My body is almost dead, and yet I have never felt so intensely alive as I feel now.' He had discovered that life was not conditioned by his body, that he was not his body, although his body was him, that he had a reality that the death of his body could not destroy.

This is a very important experience, because it is something which we must do in the course of all our life, all the time, if we want to be aware of the power of eternal life within us, and therefore unafraid, whatever happens to the temporary life which is also ours. It is impossible for us to look into the process of dying, because we cannot imagine what it consists of. But we can turn to the experience of some who have gone through an experience of communion with a dying person.

My last example is taken from the experience of a young man in his late teens or early twenties, who was asked to spend the night by the side of an old woman who was dying. She had never believed in anything except material things. And now she was going. When this young man came in the evening she was already unconscious. He sat next to her bed and prayed: prayed as best he could, with words of prayer, with the silence of prayer, with a sense of awe, a sense of compassion, and also with a deep sense of bewilderment. What was happening to this woman who was entering into a world which she had always denied, which she had never perceived? She was earth, so how could she enter into heaven? And this is what he perceived - or thought he perceived – as he communed with this old woman in compassion and bewilderment.

There was a first period when this woman lay still. And then it became clear to him through what she said, through her exclamations, her movements, that she was seeing something, and what she saw – from her words – were figures of darkness, the powers of evil that were crowding round her bed, claiming her as their own – beings which were nearest the earth because they were fallen. Then suddenly she turned and said that she saw light, that the darkness that was pressing on all sides and the figures of evil that were compassing her about, were gradually receding and she saw beings of light. And she cried for mercy, saying, 'I don't belong, but save me!' And then she said, 'I see the light.' And with these words, 'I see the light', she died.

****

BEREAVEMENT

As I have said, our first and most continuous contact with death is through bereavement. It is by learning to live through and to understand the death of others, in them and in ourselves, that we can best learn to face death and eventually face our own death, first as a possibility – indeed, a certainty, but a certainty which is often apparently so far removed from us that we do not call it a certainty – and then as the very reality that comes upon us. So let me dwell a little more on this subject of bereavement.

I have mentioned already that one of the immediate problems which a bereaved person has to face is the experience and sense of loneliness, of being left behind by the only person who filled all the time, all the space, the whole of their heart. But even if all the heart was not involved, the person who has left us leaves behind a vast empty space. While the person is ill we give a great deal more time to thought. Our activities are centred and directed. When the person dies, however, very often those left behind feel that their activities no longer have any purpose, or at least no immediate purpose, no centre, no direction. A life that, however painful and agonising, was running like a stream, becomes a bog. Also loneliness means that there is no longer that one person with whom one can talk, whom one can listen to, to whom one can be attentive, who responds and reacts, to whom we react and respond. And the person who leaves us is more often than not the very person who gave us, in our own eyes, ultimate value: the person to whom we truly mattered, the person who asserted our existence and our importance.

I have mentioned more than once on the occasion of a wedding, the words of Léon Bloy, who says, 'To tell a person "I love you" is tantamount to saying "You shall never die."' And these words apply in the present context. The person who leaves us is no longer there to proclaim our ultimate value, our ultimate significance. The person is no longer there who can say 'I love you', and therefore you are no longer affirmed, acknowledged eternally. This is something which must be faced. It is not something which must be or can be put to one side, which can be forgotten, or evaded. A void is created, and this void should never be artificially filled with things which are unworthy of what they replace.

We must be prepared to face pain, to face agony of mind, to face all those things which go on in us and which are indeed inflicted upon us by the false goodwill of those who surround us and who continue to revive our pain and our suffering by enhancing it and insisting on it. We must be prepared to recognise that pain is one of the expressions of love, and that if we claim that we truly love the person who has now departed this life, we must be prepared to love this person in and through pain as we loved this person in and through joy, the joy of assertion, the joy of a common life.

This requires courage, and there is a great deal that needs to be explained in this respect in our present day, when so many people, in order to escape the pain, will turn to tranquillisers, to alcohol, to entertainment of one sort or another in order to forget; because what is going on in a human soul may be obscured, but continues to go on, and unless it is resolved it leaves the person the poorer, not the richer.

Something else which a person bereaved must learn never to do is to speak of the love relationship that existed before in the past tense. One should never say, 'We loved one another.' We should always say, 'We love each other.' It is important to remember the words of the Song of Solomon: 'Love is as strong as death.' Love cannot be corrupted by death. We cannot allow our love to become a thing of the past without recognising that this means that we do not believe in the continuing life of the person who has died. But then we must recognise that we are unbelievers and atheists in the crudest sense, and face it from a quite different angle: face the fact that if there is no God, if there is no eternal life, then the death which has occurred has no metaphysical significance at all. It is an event of natural history. It is a victory of the laws of physics and chemistry, and it is the return of the person to the elements of nature and of a continuing existence not as a person but as a part of nature. But we must in each case face squarely either our faith or our lack of faith and take a stand and act accordingly.

Very often those left behind feel that the loss of the person is not only their loss; it is a loss that bereaves everyone around them of something precious, of an intelligence, of a heart, of a will, of one who acted rightly and beautifully. And the bereaved one dwells also on this loss. At this point we must remember – and this is essential – that everyone who lives sets an example: an example of how to live well, or an example of how to live badly. We must learn from everyone, living or departed, that which is wrong in order to avoid it, and that which is right in order to emulate it. Everyone who has known a departed person must reflect profoundly on the mark which this person's life has set on his or her life, reflect profoundly on what kind of seed was sown by the life of this person, and let it bear fruit.

There is a saying in the Gospel that unless the seed dies it will not bear fruit, but if it dies, it will bear fruit thirtyfold, sixtyfold and a hundredfold. This is exactly what happens if we reflect with all our heart, with all our mind and memory, with all our understanding and with all our sense of justice, on the life of those who depart this life.

We must have the courage to use that sword – which is God's own sword – to divide what is light from what is darkness, to use all our discernment to sort out the tares from the wheat. And then, having collected all the wheat we are capable of discerning, each of us, every person who has known the departed person, should seek to bear fruit of his or her life, to live according to an example given and received, to emulate everything which is worthy of emulation in the life of this person.

I know that each of us is more like a twilight than bright, shining light, but the light shines in the darkness, and this light must be seen, and separated from the darkness within ourselves so that as many as have known a given person may live and bear fruit from his or her life.

At the funeral service we stand with lighted candles. In this way we are proclaiming the Resurrection: we stand with lighted candles in the same way in which we stand in church during Easter night. But we also stand witnessing before God that this person brought at least a flicker of light into the twilight of the world, that this person has not lived in vain, and that we will keep, protect, increase, share out this light, so that it may illumine more and more people, so that it may grow thirtyfold, sixtyfold, a hundredfold. And if we set out to live in such a way, as to be the continuation of the earthly life of the departed person, if we set out to be the continuation of everything that was noble and good and true and holy in this person, then truly this person will not have lived in vain. There will be no room in us for any hope of a prompt death, because we will have a function to fulfil.

To take an example which is certainly far beyond anything within our experience, think of the words of St Paul: 'For me Christ is life; death would be a gain, because as long as I live in the flesh I am separated from Christ. And yet it is more expedient for you that I should live': for where our treasure is there will our heart be also.

The treasure of St Paul was Christ, the most precious discovery and possession of his ardent and powerful soul, the love of his life which led him to long for the time when he would clothe himself with eternity and see as he is seen, know as he is known, commune without any veil or dark glass between him and the object of his love. But with all this, he knew that, having experienced what he had experienced, he could bring a message to the world which those who could speak only from hearsay could not bring. And so he was prepared to renounce the meeting he longed for, the communion and oneness he longed for, in order to bring his testimony. His love for his own people was great enough for him to exclaim that he would be prepared to be separated from Christ for ever, if that could give them access to Him. In a small measure every person who lives and who becomes our treasure or one of the most treasured possessions of our heart can, in a small way, exemplify this.

This leads me to another aspect of the same situation. We are left behind to make it possible for all we have seen, all we have heard, all we have experienced, to multiply and spread and start a new chain of light on earth. But if we can truly, sincerely say that the person who has departed this life was a treasure to us, then where our treasure is there our heart should be, and we should, together with this person who has entered into eternity, live as completely, as deeply as possible in eternity.

For this is the only place where we can be together with the departed person. It means that as more and more beloved ones leave this earthly pilgrimage and enter into the stability and the peace of life eternal, we should feel that we belong more and more to that world, ever more completely, ever more perfectly, that its values increasingly become ours. And if one of the beloved ones, one of the most treasured treasures, is called the Lord Jesus Christ, then we can truly, while we are still on earth, like St Paul, long with all our hearts and minds, with all our flesh and heart, for the day when we shall be inseparably united with Him.

Facing our own death is something which we do in ways that are very different according to our age and circumstances. Think of children who hear the word 'death', have perhaps a vague notion about it, or have perhaps lost a parent or parents and grieved in loneliness. Their perception is that of bereavement, but not of death itself. Most children, certainly most boys, at certain moments of their lives, play war games. 'I have shot you down. You are dead. Lie down.' And the child lies down and he knows at that moment emotionally, but within the security of the game, that he is dead, which means that he has no right to play, no right to run, no right to move. He must lie in a certain manner. Life continues around him, and he is no longer part of it, until at a certain moment it is too much, and he jumps up saying, 'I've had enough of being dead. It's your turn.'

This is a very important experience because the child through this experience discovers that he can be an outsider to life, and yet it is a game and he possesses the security which games possess. It may come to an end at any moment by mutual agreement, but something has been learnt. I remember an extremely sensitive child in one of our boys' camps years and years back who experienced it in such a way that he could not stand the tension. So I played a whole game with him, living, hiding, emerging from hiding and being killed with him, for him to be able to enter into this experience. For him it was not a game; it was too real.

A child may also be introduced to death in a monstrous way that will make him morbid or, on the contrary, in a sane and healthy way. What follows is a real example, not a parable. A beloved grandmother died after a long and painful illness. I was summoned to the house, and when I arrived, I discovered that the children had been removed. The parents explained, 'We could not allow the children to stay in a house where there was a dead person.' I replied, 'Why not?' 'Because they know what death is.' 'And what is death?' I asked 'They saw a rabbit torn to pieces by a cat in the garden the other day, so they know what death is.' So I suggested that if that was the image of death which these children had they were bound all their lives to live with a sense of horror whenever they heard the word death, whenever they attended a memorial service, whenever they saw a coffin – untold horror hidden in a wooden box.

After a long argument, during which the parents said to me that the children were bound to become nervous wrecks if they were allowed to see their grandmother and that their mental condition would be my responsibility, I brought the children back. Their first question was, 'What really happened to Granny?' I replied, 'You have heard her say time and again that she longed to join her husband in God's kingdom, where he had already gone. Now it has happened to her.' 'So she is happy?' said one of the children. I said, 'Yes.' Then we went into the room where the grandmother lay. The stillness was wonderful. The old lady, whose face had been ravaged by the last years of suffering, lay absolutely still and serene. One of the children said, 'So that is death.' And the other one said, 'How beautiful.' Here are two forms of the same experience. Are we going to allow children to see death in terms of the little rabbit torn to pieces by cats in the garden, or are we going to let them see the serenity and beauty of death?

In the Orthodox Church we bring the dead person to the church as soon as we can. We pray in the presence of an open coffin. Adults and children approach it. Death is not something to be hidden: it is something simple and a part of life. And the children can look into the face of the departed person and see the peace which has come upon it. We give a kiss to the departed person. This is the moment when we must not forget to warn the child that when he or she kisses the forehead of a person that was always warm it will be cold and we can say, 'This is the mark of death.' Life goes with warmth. Death is cold. And then the child is not horrified, because it has experience of things cold and things warm, and each of them has its own nature, each of them has its own meaning.

These first impressions determine how we later confront death later on. In our youth we may be confronted with death in a tragic way – violent death, accident, war. I remember a young man who had never given a thought to death in his life, whose friend was killed in a motorcycle accident. He came to see me and he said that when he saw what folly had done – the body of his friend, broken, torn – it had made him think. The thought that came to him seemed to me a complete *non sequitur*. It seemed to me something that had nothing to do with what had happened. His thought was, 'By not becoming a saint I am robbing God of his glory and my neighbour of his due.' The death – brutal, violent, ugly – which he had witnessed had placed him face to face with values eternal and absolute which he carried within him but which had always been dormant, untapped, unused.

In war death is met at times with terror and at times with elation. But it is so often met by people of an age and in conditions which have not prepared them for death, for dying, for confrontation with death. Young, vigorous human bodies devoid of any seed of death as it seems to them, within a few moments are confronted with the possibility – at times the certainty – of dying. Reactions may be very different: much depends on what you were fighting for, whether you fought with conviction or through necessity, forced into the struggle or having chosen to fight. And it is not the nobility of the cause, it is the wholeheartedness with which you gave your assent and your life to it that will determine the way in which you die.

I remember two horribly wounded young German soldiers in 1940, who were very close to their death. I came up to them and asked one of them, 'Are you suffering greatly?' He looked at me with his dying eyes and said, 'I don't feel any suffering. We are beating you.' He could face death from within the certainty that he was doing the right thing. To me he was doing the wrong thing. But that was not the point: the incentive for his actions was wholehearted.

At other times dying is different. Another soldier, a young father who was leaving behind his wife and his farm, said to me, 'I shall die tonight. I am sad to leave my wife on her own, but that can't be helped. But I am so afraid of dying alone.' And I said to him that he would not die alone. I would sit with him, and that as long as he could be aware of me by opening his eyes, or by speaking, I would not leave him. This I did, and he held my hand, and from time to time he would squeeze it to be sure I was there. And so we sat, and he died in peace and was spared the loneliness of death.

On the other hand, at times God grants someone a lonely death which is not a death of loneliness but which is an aloneness together with God, who has made sure that no-one in a foolish, dramatic way will break through and bring anguish, fear, despair to a soul that can freely enter into eternity.

****

DEATH

I will now turn to the problem of the reality of death and the various services which relate to it in the Orthodox Church. As anyone can read them or experience them, I will not go into detail, but will only single out a certain number of characteristics. First of all, there are two main services: the short service in memory of the departed – the Panikhida – and the funeral service of lay people. There are other services which are less familiar – the Canon which is read when possible over a person who is departing this life and whose departure is difficult, hard. There is also the service for the funeral of a child, and that of a priest. I want to single out a certain number of basic features which are common to all.

There are two sides to these services: a concern for the soul and a concern for the body. We have in common with all churches this prayerful concern for the departing soul or the departed soul. But I believe that in Orthodoxy the attention paid to the body, the attitude which we have to the body, is both very special and very significant. In the Panikhida all our attention is concentrated on the soul that is now in eternity face to face with the Living God, growing into an ever-deepening knowledge of God, and an ever-deepening communion with Him. In the funeral service, together with this concern for the departed soul which somehow is still so close to the earth, there is a deep concern for the body.

In the funeral service we find that the body is seen from two angles. On the one hand we are aware that the earthly body is doomed to corruption: 'Dust thou art and unto dust shalt thou return'; there is acute pain in the thought of this, and there is an acute pain in the sight of this bodily corruption.

My mother died on Good Friday; she was buried almost a week later. On the morning of the funeral I went to spend a last moment with her in the chapel of our Parish House, and for the first time I saw the marks of corruption on her hands and on her face. And it hurt me deeply that these hands which I had loved, this face which I had loved, were now beginning to show corruption. My first movement was to turn away and not look; not to turn away from my mother, but to avoid seeing these spreading black marks. But then I felt that there was here a last message which I had to look at and understand. This body which had been so dear was now going to disintegrate, to become dust. The message to me was this: 'If you want never to lose me, do not come and wait for me at my grave. What will be left of me which is earthly will be there and you can cherish the spot and you can look at it, but our communion is not through the body any more; our communion is in God.'

I said this to the Parish, and I was rebuked by some for being crude and insensitive, but it was something which I could say only when it was *my* mother who had died. I could not have said it when someone else's mother or wife or brother or friend had died. I believe we must find, in our attitude to the departed, this balance between the acceptance of reality and the certainty of our faith, between the sight of corruption and the certainty of eternal life, between the love for the place where what is left of a much loved body rests and the certainty that the relationship of communion continues in God in eternity. We find in the various prayers, in the Troparion and the Canon, in the hymns of St John Damascene, a reflection of this pain and this sense of tragedy – a human body that was called to eternal life, slain by mortality born of the loss of God.

On the other hand, Holy Scripture uses the word 'body', or 'person', or 'soul' on occasions to signify the whole person. Indeed the connection between the body and the soul, between the body and spiritual experience itself, is total, complete. We have the testimony of St Paul saying to us that 'faith comes by hearing, and hearing by the word of God' – a word spoken, a word heard, both through bodily means: the lips of the speaker, the ears of the hearer – and yet it reaches the heart, the mind, the very core of a person in such a way that one word of God can transform the life of a person. We know how much all our senses participate in every movement of the mind, of the heart, how much love is expressed by a mother to a small child through touch; how much consolation can be given by the touch of a hand, how much love in all its forms finds expression through the body. And so, if we look at the body of a departed person, we do not see – as many try at least to say to console themselves to blot out the pain – a piece of discarded clothing . It is not clothing, and it is not discarded. It is a body which is as real, as really the person, as the soul. It is only body and soul together that makes a complete person.

This is brought out in a strange and unexpected way, by St Isaac the Syrian, who, speaking of the body, says that the eternal destiny of man cannot be fixed before the resurrection of the body, because the body has as much right as the soul to choose and to determine the eternal destiny of the person – words which are mysterious to us because we cannot imagine how that can be. And yet, this body is me as much as my soul is me. It is only in their togetherness that I can be seen. And so when we look at this body, we look at it with veneration. We see in it all the suffering and all the joy, all the mystery of life that has been that person. The body could be called the visible of the invisible. In that sense perhaps it is not in vain that in Slavonic, in the church services, we use for the body the word *moshchi*, which is the same word we use for relics. Every body surrounded with love and veneration, called to the resurrection, a body that was instrumental during the course of a whole life in the mysterious communion with God through baptism, through chrismation, through anointing with the oil of the sick, through communion in the Body and Blood of Christ, through the reception of blessings – every such body is, as it were, a seed 'sown in corruption that it may rise in glory'. This body of corruption, of which St Paul wanted to be freed in order to live fully face to face with God, is at the same time called to eternity.

And so, on the one hand we see this body as something dear and precious, wounded and conquered by mortality, subjected to death. And on the other hand we see it as a seed sown in order to rise again in the glory of immortality through the resurrection. Looking at it we cannot help seeing its connection with the Body of Christ. St Paul used the phrase 'Our life is hid with Christ in God'. Our bodily humanity is hid in the mystery of the Trinity, and this bodily humanity comprises our humanity. In Christ, in the Mother of God, we can see what our body is called to be: a glorious body. So we are not divided but find ourselves in a complex situation in which, heartbroken that we are separated, we look in wonder at the fact that a human body can die, and in faith and hope at a body which one day will rise like Christ's.

And now the soul. There are several prayers that precede the death of a person, that are connected with preparation for death. First of all there is the turning from things temporal to things eternal. St Seraphim could say before his death: 'Bodily I am nearing death, and in spirit I am like one just born,' with all the newness, all the freshness of a beginning, not a finishing.

This leads to the necessity for preparing for death through a stern and liberating process of coming to terms with life, making one's peace with everyone, with oneself, with one's conscience, with one's circumstances, with the present and the past, with events and with people – and indeed with the future, the coming of death itself. There must be a process by which we come to make our peace, as I think St Isaac of Syria puts it, with God, with our conscience, with our neighbour, even with the things which we have handled. So that the whole earth can say to us, 'Go in peace', and so that we can say to all that the earth was to us, 'Stay in peace and may God's peace and blessing be on you.' One cannot enter into eternity tied and fettered by hatred. If we want to be able, in the short time which the coming of death offers us, to do all this, it is essential that we should consider all our life as an ascent, an ascent into eternity, not a gradual process of decay and descent towards death, but an ascent to the moment when through the narrow gate of death we shall enter into eternity – not divesting ourselves of temporal life, but clothing ourselves with eternity, to use the words of St Paul.

If, in the Panikhida, there is a primary concentration of attention on the departed soul, attention is, of course, also paid to the departing of the soul in the funeral service. According to Orthodox tradition, for the first three days after the death of a person, his or her soul remains close to the earth, visiting familiar places perhaps, recalling to memory all that the earth had been; so that it is in full possession of all its memories that a soul will leave the earth and stand before God. We mark these three days with particular attention. Prayers are offered, panikhidas are celebrated, our thought concentrates upon all the complexities of our relationship with the departed person. And we too have our part to play, for we too must untie knots within our soul. We must also be able from the depth of our heart and of all our being to say to the departed person, 'Forgive me,' and also say, 'I forgive you, go in peace.'

Perhaps it is here that we find the meaning of the old saying that one should not speak ill of the departed. If we had truly, in all truth, said to the person who has departed this life, 'I set you free; I will stand before God proclaiming forgiveness, let nothing that has happened between us stand in your way to fulfilment and eternal joy', then how can we go back and remember evil, past bitterness? This is not a way of closing one's eyes to reality, because if there really has been evil between us and the departed person, then how much we must pray to God to set both free – ourselves and the other – to hear the words of forgiveness, 'Go in peace', and to repeat these words with an ever-increasing depth of understanding, with an ever-increasing awareness of a growing freedom.

There are passages in this burial service which we can find difficult. To start this service with the words 'Blessed is our God' requires all our faith and all our determination. At times it stretches our faith to the limit. 'The Lord gave, the Lord hath taken away. Blessed be the

Name of the Lord', said Job. But it is not an easy thing when our hearts are broken and when we see the person whom we love above all dead before our eyes.

And then there are prayers which are prayers of faith and prayers of human frailty – prayers of faith accompanying the soul of the departed person, offered before the face of God as a testimony of love; because this is what prayers for the departed are: a testimony before God that this person has not lived in vain. However sinful and frail, this person has left behind a loving memory: everything else will become dust. Love will survive all things. Faith and hope will go when faith is replaced by vision and hope by possession, but love will never go.

As we stand and pray for the departed, all we say is 'Lord, this person has not lived in vain. What he or she has left on earth is an example and is love; the example we shall follow; the love will never die.' To proclaim before God our undying love for the dead person is a way of affirming this person, not only in time, but in eternity. When we stand with lighted candles at the service we indeed proclaim our faith in the Resurrection, but we also proclaim before the face of God that this person has brought a light into the world. 'Let your light so shine before all men, that seeing your good works they may give glory to your Father, who is in heaven.' We proclaim that this person has not just shone a creative light, has not just impressed us by genius, by beauty or talent alone, but has allowed the light of God, the uncreated divine glory, to shine forth. And this is something that will never die on earth.

Heartbroken we may well be, yet we still proclaim these words of faith: 'Blessed is our God, always, now and for ever and to the ages of ages.' At times, even more tragically, we sing the Troparion of the Resurrection: 'Christ is risen from the dead; by death He has undone death, and to those in the tombs He has given life', when before our eyes lies the dead body of a person whom we love. But there is also the voice of the Church speaking to us words of comfort and consolation: 'Blessed is the way thou treadest today, O human soul, for a place of rest has been prepared for thee', and 'My soul lives and I give glory unto the Lord.'

All the pain which we rightly experience, is expressed on behalf of the dying person in one of the troparia of the Canon for the soul that has difficulty in departing from life: 'How painful it is to think of our separation', says the soul.

Yet, there is also our certainty that death, which is our bereavement, is a birth into eternity, that death is a beginning and not and end, that it is a great and holy encounter between God and the living soul, which can be fulfilled only in God.

****

METROPOLITAN ANTHONY OF SOUROZH
A biographical note

Metropolitan Anthony of Sourozh was born Andrei Bloom in 1914, in Lausanne, into a family of diplomats and soldiers. His mother was the half-sister of the composer Alexander Scriabin. The 1917 revolution overtook the family in Persia, and they set off for Europe hoping to settle in England, but a leaking ship landed them in Marseilles.

Like so many other White Russian exiles, the future bishop and his family knew real deprivation in Paris. A loving and devoted family and the Russian youth movement relieved the harshness of the boy's schooldays. A tough survivor, Andrei Bloom found God at 15. He studied medicine, qualifying as a surgeon, with a doctorate in oncology. He served in the French army and then in the Resistance as a surgeon. In 1943 he professed monastic vows, taking the name Anthony. He practised as a doctor among the poorest, most marginalised Paris Russians, whilst also teaching in the Russian Gymnasium.

In 1948 the retiring chaplain of the ecumenical Fellowship of St Alban and St Sergius pressed him to come to London. Father Anthony saw this as a call that he had no right to refuse. Until he learned spoken English he conducted his work at the Fellowship in Authorised Version biblical language. In 1956 he became the vicar of the Russian parish in London, and was soon welcoming the English partners of his younger parishioners. For him Orthodoxy was not an ethnically circumscribed faith, but a revelation of the wonder of Christianity. He became widely known and there is hardly a cathedral or major city church which has not invited Metropolitan Anthony to preach or conduct retreats. He also spoke in hospitals, medical schools and hospices.

Unlike many in the diaspora, Metropolitan Anthony remained faithful to the martyred Mother Church in Russia. In 1957 he was consecrated bishop, and in 1962 archbishop and Exarch (primate) of all the Moscow Patriarchal parishes in Western Europe. In 1966 he was elevated to the rank of Metropolitan. He has been awarded honorary doctorates by the universities of Aberdeen (1973) and Cambridge (1996), as well as the Theological Academies of Moscow and Kiev.